German Motorcy

A VISUAL HISTORY IN VINTAGE PHOTOS AND RESTORED EXAMPLES, PART 1

by David Doyle

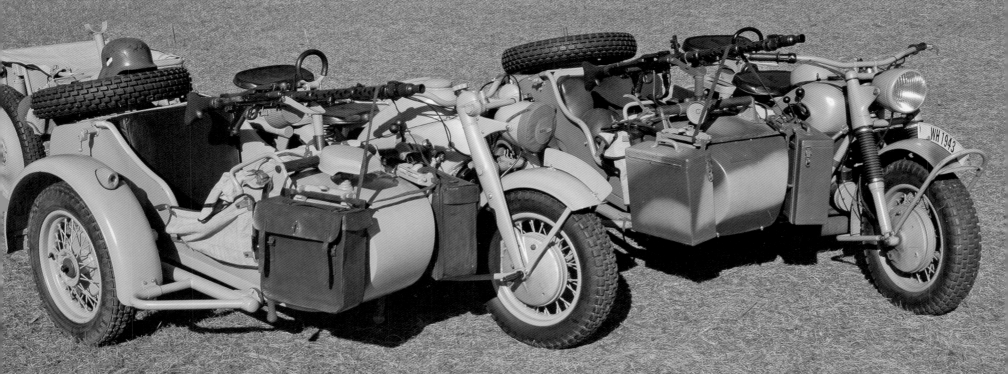

BMW R4 • R12 • R35 • R71 • R74 and Zündapp KS750

Published by
Ampersand Group, Inc.
In cooperation with HobbyLink Japan **HobbyLink Japan**
235 NE 6th Ave., Suite B
Delray Beach, FL 33483-5543
561-266-9686 • 561-266-9786 Fax
www.ampersandpubco.com • www.hlj.com

Acknowledgements:

This book would not have been possible without the generous assistance of Brian Slark and the staff of the Barber Motorsports Museum in Leeds, Alabama; Tom Kailbourn; John Blackman; Doug Mitchel; Hans Devos; Jack Wells; Kent Berg; Victor Vick; Chris Hughes; Pat Ware; Ian Le Riche; Roger Condron, Scott Taylor; the WWII Victory Museum in Auburn, Indiana; the Karl Smith collection and numerous bike owners who choose to remain anonymous. My wonderful wife Denise never failed to help and assist in every way needed. Thank you to you all.

All unattributed contemporary photos are copyright of the author.
All unattributed vintage photos are copyright of The Ampersand Group, Inc.

Sources:

BMW Motorcycles in WWII, R12/R75 by Janusz Piekalkiewicz,
Schiffer Publishing, Atglen, PA, 1991

Motorcycles of the Wehrmacht, a Photo Chronicle, by Horst Hinrichsen,
Schiffer Publishing, Atglen, PA, 1994

German Military Motorcycles of the Reichswehr and Wehrmacht 1934-1945 by
Horst Hinrichsen, Schiffer Publishing, Atglen, PA, 1977

German Motorcycles in World War II, BMW, DKW, NSU, Triumph, Viktoria
and Zündapp by Stefan Knittel, Schiffer Publishing, Atglen, PA, 1990

Heavy Sidecar Motorcycles of the Wehrmacht, 1935-1945,
by Horst Hinrichsen, Schiffer Publishing, Atglen, PA, 2001

Cover: At the outset of WWII, armies worldwide made use of motorcycles, from messenger service to reconnaissance, but German forces relied more upon the motorcycle, and arguably used them more successfully, than anyone else. From the lightweight BMW R4 to the heavyweight R75 and KS750, so sought after were motorcycles that many civilian bikes were confiscated and impressed to supplement purpose-built military machines like this R12. (Doug Mitchel)

Rear cover: Luftwaffe troops prepare to resume an advance on Zündapp KS750 motorcycles with sidecars. The sidecars are equipped with holders for Jerrycan liquid containers. The nearest motorcycle bears license plate number WL-276517.

Title page: Two legendary, restored German heavy motorcycles with powered sidecars sit side by side. To the left is a Zündapp KS750 in an overall dark yellow paint scheme and towing a light trailer, and to the right is a BMW R75 in a dark yellow and dark gray camouflage scheme.

Right: A German soldier poses for his photo on a very muddy BMW R75 motorcycle, license number WH-495442, at a settlement most likely on the Eastern Front. This heavy motorcycle was a workhorse of the German armed forces in World War II.

Table of Contents

Introduction

Starting in 1928, the German Reichswehr began training with private motorcycle clubs for the execution of a variety of independent tasks, much in the same manner as the traditional cavalry. The use of private clubs was necessary as the Treaty of Versailles forbade motorized combat troops. These groups provided extensive practical experience in the development and deployment of this new type of unit.

The Kradschützentruppe (loosely translated as motorcycle troops) was officially created as an independent branch of service of the German armed forces in 1935. Independent battalions (Kradschützenbataillone) were created, each consisting of three companies (Kradschützenkompanien). Infantry regiments had two companies, while armored reconnaissance units each had a single company. The companies were divided into three platoons (Kradschützenzüge) each with three squads (Kradschützen). These squads would typically be made up of grenadiers, but two squads would form a heavy group armed with MG 34 machine guns and ammunition. Each company was also assigned a light cross-country car and a repair truck. The typical complement of motorcycles was 54 sidecar combinations and five single motorcycles.

The major tasks of the Kradschützen were mopping-up for the following troops and employment as an advance guard, surprise raid-like attacks against an opponent's flanks and rear, as well as pursuit of the opponent.

Although they were highly specialized motorized troops, the Kradschützen were considered a branch of the infantry. When assigned to an infantry element, the battalions acted as independent and special components of the infantry. In armored reconnaissance units they served as a motorized infantry unit or as an infantry component in clearing-up operations.

Their training stressed not only the specialized nature of their roles as mobile troops, but it also had the same elements as regular infantry training. Training regularly included 40km road marches on foot as well as their motorized training. Kradschützen candidates were selected for endurance and toughness. Speed, mobility and familiarity with the cross-country capabilities of their Beiwagenkräder (sidecar combinations) were particularly and intensively practiced. The special motorized training of the Kradschützen stressed proficiency in driving in low light situations, with varying loads in the sidecars, in bad weather conditions (frost, snow, ice), as well as over difficult terrain. Contests and exhibitions were also encouraged to allow individual riders to demonstrate their prowess with their machines.

A motorized element of the pioneer troops was also formed. Called the "Kradschützensteg," they trained for the creation and elimination of road blocks, building auxiliary bridges, overcoming small obstacles and the creation of minor field fortifications.

With the creation of the Kradschützentruppe, they were initially equipped with the BMW R11 and R12-Beiwagenkräder. The lighter and less durable R11 was considered only a temporary solution and was gradually completely replaced by the R12. In addition to the two BMW machines, the Zündapp K800W and KS600W were also used solo and as Beiwagenkräder. The K800W had cooling problems that were eliminated with the KS600W model. However, by 1937, it became clear that heavier and more powerful motorcycles would be needed. Specifications were laid down and BMW responded with its R75 model and Zündapp with its KS750 model. Both vehicles were conceived as heavy Beiwagenkräder with drive shafts for their sidecars, a 26-hp engine (as opposed to 18-hp on the R12), a reverse gear and greater ground clearance under the sidecar.

As all the Beiwagenkräder had originated from civilian production and differed only in the headlight covers and military paint, it was found that the machines simply did not meet the harsh mechanical requirements of wartime use. This was especially true of those machines employed on the Russian and North African fronts.

As a result, the Kradschützenfahrzeuge Beiwagenkrädern were gradually replaced by the Kübelwagen, Schwimmwagen and Sd.Kfz. 250 half-tracked armored personnel carriers during the years 1942-43. The use of motorcycles by dispatch riders (Kradmelder) as both single machines or as Beiwagenkrädern continued to the war's end.

Above: A BMW R75 is seen here being used in the harsh conditions of the Eastern Front during the winter of 1943-44. The rider has arranged the lower portion of his "Kradmantel" rubberized coat to direct heat from the cylinder heads to his upper body. **Right:** The German army motorcycle rifle companies of WWII, such as this one, can perhaps be compared to the cavalry. Fast, mobile and well-armed, these units were a key part of Germany's "Blitzkrieg" technique. Less sensational, but no less important, was the extensive use of motorcycle messengers during the war. (NARA, both)

BMW R4

BMW began producing its R4 motorcycle in 1932 as an economy model. There was a civilian and a military model, with the military one differing from the civilian with the addition of a skidpan and different saddlebag brackets. BMW produced over 15,000 R4s in five successive series from 1932 to 1937, with most going to the Wehrmacht. This important military sale helped BMW survive the Great Depression. Powering the R4 was a single-cylinder, four-stroke, 398cc engine. The first series of the R4 had the M69S1 engine, which developed 12 horsepower at 3,500 rpm. The fifth-series engine, M69S5, produced 14 horsepower at 4,000 rpm. The Wehrmacht used the R4 extensively in the 1930s for training purposes.

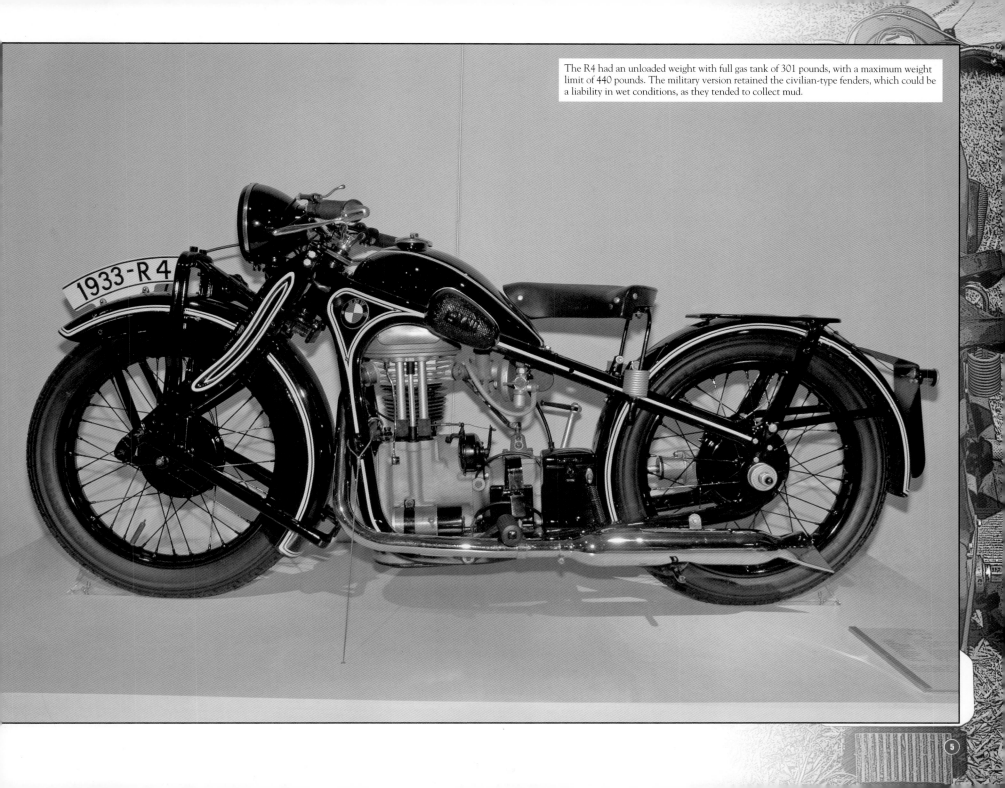

The R4 had an unloaded weight with full gas tank of 301 pounds, with a maximum weight limit of 440 pounds. The military version retained the civilian-type fenders, which could be a liability in wet conditions, as they tended to collect mud.

The wheelbase of the R4 was 51.18" and the overall length was 77.95".

1933 - R4

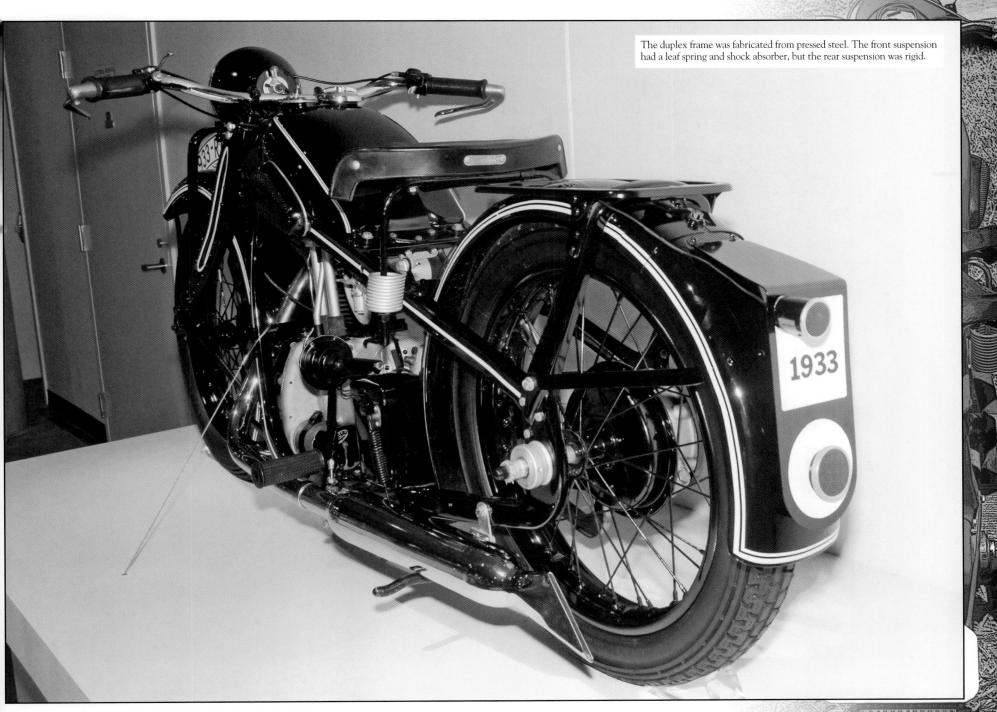

The duplex frame was fabricated from pressed steel. The front suspension had a leaf spring and shock absorber, but the rear suspension was rigid.

1933

Left: The fender, main fork, and frame of the R4 sports decidedly nonmilitary pin striping. The BMW logo plate on the frame below the fuel tank is affixed with two slotted screws, one on each side. The handlebar and levers and the fuel-tank cap are chromed. **Top right:** The front suspension is shown in close-up. Over the fender is the leaf spring and spring fork, with friction shock absorbers on both sides. These shocks were added during production and included large knobs to adjust the tension. **Above right:** A BMW logo plate with its distinctive blue and white circle design is attached to the frame with two slotted screws. In wartime photographs, sometimes these plates are seen in their original colors, and sometimes they have been painted over.

The single, vertical cylinder of the engine is close behind the front of the frame. The single carburetor, model SUM CK 3/500 Fr, is to the right, with part of the left knee guard visible above it. At the bottom is the Bosch generator.

A close-up view shows the carburetor and air filter as well as fuel lines. At the top is the underside of the fuel tank. The kick-starter is at the bottom center.

The rear support for the seat and the left coil spring for it are clearly visible from this perspective. The knee guard (upper left) has a cross-hatched texture and features the initials BMW on it.

The BMW R4 was shaft-drive. A close-up view shows the right side of the rear wheel and spokes, as well as the differential, drum brake, brake lever, and brake actuating rod. The rear tire measured 26-3.5, and the brake was 7.08" in diameter.

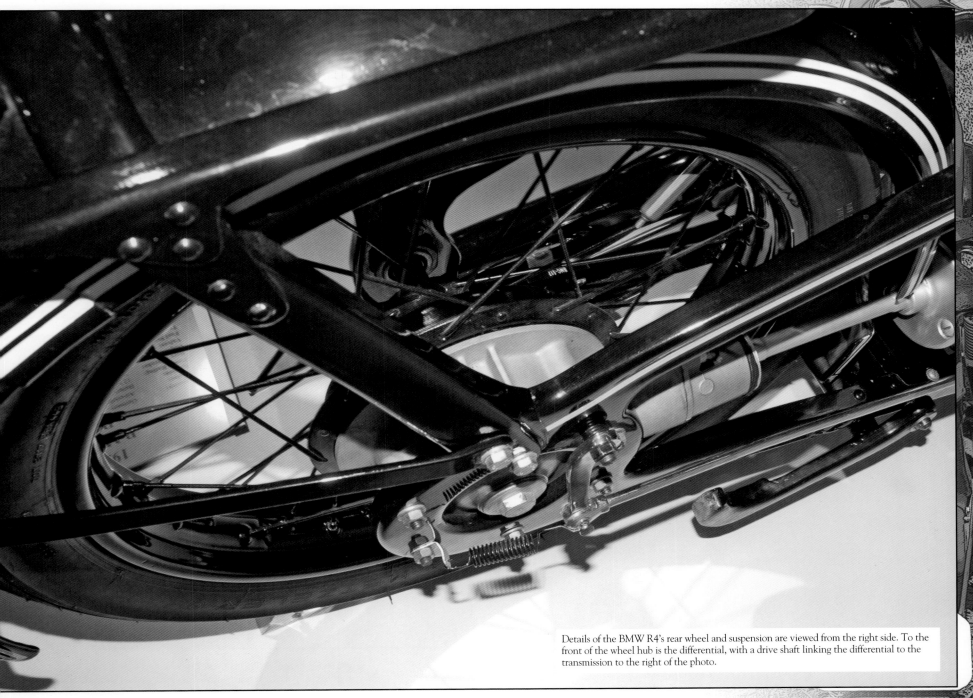

Details of the BMW R4's rear wheel and suspension are viewed from the right side. To the front of the wheel hub is the differential, with a drive shaft linking the differential to the transmission to the right of the photo.

Left: The arrangements of the main fork and the spring fork are shown. Between the forks is the adjustment knob of the right shock absorber. Attached to the bottom of the fork is the front kickstand, or crutch. **Top right:** Details of the front suspension are emphasized in this close-up. The front ends of the leaf spring and the two friction shock absorbers that flank it are secured to the spring fork (right). The rear links of the shocks are attached to the fork.

Above right: A close-up of the front wheel from the right side displays the patterns of the spokes and the design of the brake drum. The front kickstand, coming in from the lower left, is fastened to the bottom of the fork with large hex screws.

BMW R12

The BMW R12 was the successor to the BMW R4, with both military and civilian touring versions. Some 36,000 of these heavy motorcycles were produced from 1935 to 1942. With an unloaded weight with full fuel tank of 407 pounds and a maximum weight limit of 660 pounds, a 740cc side-valve, four-stroke, flat-twin engine producing 18 horsepower at 3,400 rpm powered the R4. The R4 could be operated solo or with an unpowered seitenwagen (sidecar). Here, an R12 gets a push while fording a stream in the central sector of the Eastern Front in the summer of 1942. Foliage and what appear to be pieces of camouflage netting have been strategically placed on the vehicle. (BA 009-0870-23A)

Three soldiers on a BMW R12 with a sidecar pose for the photographer during a winter exercise or operation. Over the front fender is license plate WH-166379. A unit or tactical symbol is painted on the fender below the license plate. Note the smooth surface of the front tire, which would not have provided ideal traction on the snow.

Motorcycle troops relax for a moment next to the same BMW R12 seen in the preceding photo, license number WH-16639. This was a circa 1936-37 R12 that was conscripted from civilian to military use. Note the saddlebag bracket on the sidecar to the front of the door.

This BMW R12 is a late-production example that was built for the Wehrmacht. The motorcycle is painted overall in a light color and the vehicle is mud-spattered, including the license plate.

Soldiers help push a BMW R12 motorcycle and sidecar through soupy mud. "PK" (for Propaganda Kompanie—probably a photographic unit) is marked on the headlight cover, and a large letter K is on the front fender. The license plate number is WH-408832. A canvas cover is secured over the sidecar, with cutouts in it to fit around the grab handle. An insignia featuring a duck in a tank is on the front of the sidecar. (NARA)

Top left: A column of BMW R12s with sidecars, from Waffen-SS Panzer Division "Das Reich," struggles along a deeply rutted trail. The closest motorcycle has the license number SS-46327. Below the license plate is the tactical symbol for a motorcycle platoon with the number 3 next to it. **Top right:** In a photograph related to the preceding one, all available hands are required to help push and pull motorcycles, including a BMW R12 with sidecar in the foreground, along a muddy, deeply rutted trail. The lead motorcycle has the number 3 next to the tactical sign for a reconnaissance motorcycle company on the sidecar and the front fender. **Above left:** An SS trooper in the sidecar attached to the BMW R12 in the foreground (SS-46328) adjusts the MG 34 mounted on the sidecar. These vehicles have the tactical sign for a motorcycle platoon with the number 3 to the right of them. **Above right:** Waffen-SS motorcycle troopers perform maintenance on the wheels of BMW R12 license number SS-46303. During operations in muddy conditions it was necessary to frequently clean and lubricate the working parts of the wheels to keep them from binding up and to prevent undue wear. (NARA, all)

The driver of a BMW R12 motorcycle with a sidecar is being assisted through a muddy stretch of road by other motorcycle troopers. An round object that at first glance appears to be above the center of the handlebar is actually a gas-mask holder that the driver is wearing. (NARA)

Top left: Waffen-SS motorcycle troops take a break along a street during a campaign. The closest motorcycle is a BMW R12 with a sidecar. On its front fender is license plate number SS-46280. Wrapped up in the bedroll strapped to the rear of the sidecar is an antiaircraft-type tripod for a machine gun. **Above left:** In a photo probably related to the preceding one, Waffen SS troops are prepared to move out of a village on a BMW R12 (SS-46315) with sidecar.

This example of an R12 has been equipped with a crash bar, which offered a degree of extra protection to the engine in the event of an accident. **Right:** A BMW R12 motorcycle with a sidecar accompanies a marching band as German forces cross the border into Sudetenland on 2 October 1938, during the German annexation of that region of Czechoslovakia. Another motorcycle and sidecar are partially visible to the far right. (NARA, all)

Left: Unshaved, road-worn SS troopers pause for their photo on a BMW R12 motorcycle with sidecar. Faintly visible in the glare on the front of the sidecar is the skull-and-crossbones symbol of Waffen-SS Panzer Division "Totenkopf." BMW logo plates in their original colors are affixed to the side of the sidecar and the frame below the fuel tank of the motorcycle. The license plate number is SS-55672. **Right:** A Waffen-SS BMW R12 with a sidecar was photographed in a shop. This vehicle has temporary white markings on the fuel tank. Details are visible of the luggage rack and straps and, to its sides, the clamps for attaching saddlebags. (NARA, both)

Mobility on even moderately muddy roads was a perennial problem for motorcycles. Here, SS motorcycle troops push their motorcycle-sidecar combinations along such a road. The nearest vehicle, SS-61163, is a BMW R12. A death's head symbol, Waffen-SS Panzer Division "Totenkopf," is present on the front of the sidecar. (NARA)

In a photo likely related to the preceding two, motorcycle troops push a BMW R12 and sidecar along a rutted, muddy trail. The symbol of the "Totenkopf" Division is on the rear of the sidecar. Below the license plate is the rectangular tactical symbol for a rifle unit. (NARA)

A soldier performs repairs or maintenance on the engine of a BMW R12 motorcycle secured to a railroad flatcar. Note the temporary markings roughly painted on the top of the fuel tank: apparently railroad shipping markings. Tools are laid out on the cover over the rider's compartment of the sidecar. The BMW logo plate below the front of the fuel tank has been painted over. (NARA)

A wider view shows the same soldier working on a BMW R12 secured to a flatcar to the rear of a Kübelwagen. To ship a motorcycle on a flatcar, the wheels were chocked and heavy wires were secured from the vehicle to the flatcar. (NARA)

The R12 was 82.67" long, with a wheelbase of 54.33". It stood 37" high and was 35.43" wide without the sidecar. (Doug Mitchel)

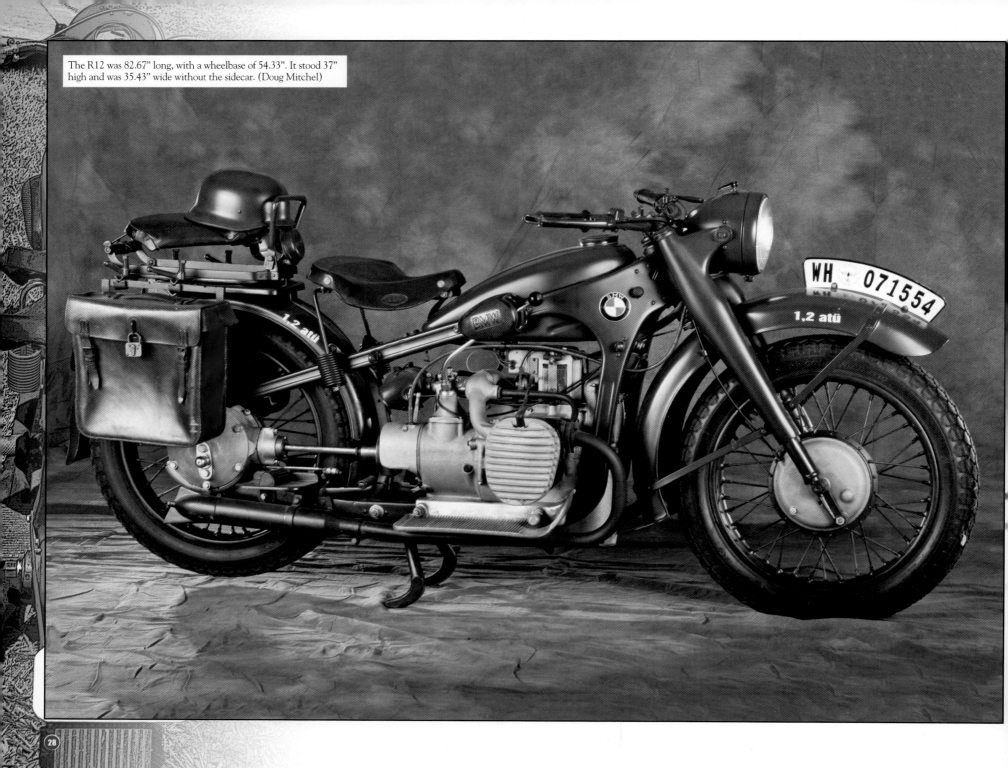

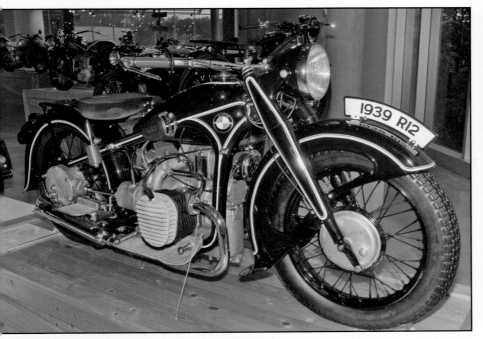

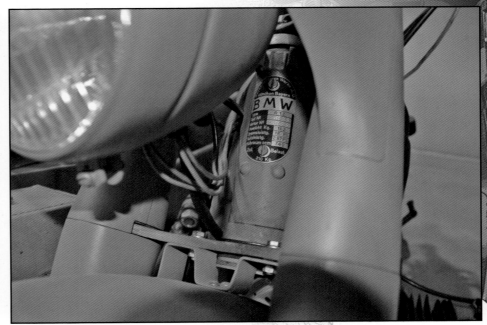

Top left: Another R12 exhibits civilian-type fenders, which were notorious mud collectors. A luggage rack is mounted over the rear fender in lieu of a passenger's saddle, but the bright-metal passenger's footrests remain in place. **Top right:** Unlike the R4 with its leaf spring and shock-absorbers front suspension, the R12 featured a telescoping fork with internal shock absorbers and coil springs. The front drum brakes were 7.87" in diameter, fully enclosed, and of the internal-ex-panding type. **Above left:** The same area of another R12 is shown. The horn was mounted on the front of the frame, facing forward. Attached to the top front of the frame on both sides of the motorcycle was a placard with the BMW logo. **Above right:** The vehicle's data plate was affixed to the front of the head tube. This plate identifies the chassis and engine numbers as 36683 and provides other specifications, including weight (162 kg.) and engine displacement (740cc).

Top left: Viewing from the front of the handlebar, the driver's saddle, gearshift, and fuel tank and filler cap are at the center. To the left on the handlebar are the front brake lever, throttle control/hand grip, headlight dimmer switch (bright chrome), and horn button. **Top right:** The construction of the civilian-type rear fender is illustrated. The twin-loop frame of the BMW R12 was made of pressed steel. The rear suspension is rigid, and the tail light assembly was attached to an L-shaped bracket on the rear of the fender. **Above left:** The R12 was powered by the M56S6 or M56S12 engine. The motorcycle came in single-carburetor and dual-carburetor versions. This vehicle has the single-carburetor configuration, with the SUM three-fuel-jet carburetor appearing toward the upper right. **Above right:** The left cylinder-head cover has a dull aluminum finish. Near its top is its part number in raised figures, OZ74. On top of it is a rubber spark plug cover. The remainder of the cylinder is a dull black, as is the left exhaust pipe. To the rear of the engine, the transmission has a dark metallic finish.

On this BMW R12 motorcycle in civilian livery, the exhaust and muffler are chromed, and the engine and the transmission are an aluminum color. Driver and passenger's footboards are installed. An oval Drilastic manufacturer's plate is affixed to the side of the driver's saddle.

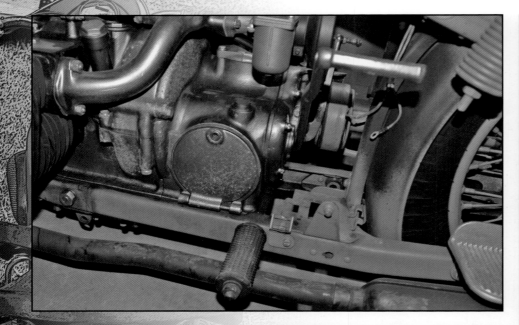

Top left: A tool kit was a standard accessory of the R12, and the kit was stored in a compartment built into the transmission casing. The circular plate with a hinge at the bottom at the center of the photo is the door for the tool kit compartment. **Above left:** A civilian-type fender for a BMW R12 is shown, with built-in fender supports instead of the thin, fastened-on supports found on R12s built for the military. Note the flared bottom rear of the fender.

The tire is a size 4.00-19. **Right:** The right side of the engine installation of a BMW R12 in civilian livery is shown. The horn, which sports a chrome finish, is mounted on the front of the frame to the rear of the fender. Built into the right kneepad is the hand shift lever, and embossed on the lower part of the chromed shift gate are the numbers 1 and 3.

Details on the right side of a BMW R12 engine and transmission are displayed. The curved footboard tended to guard the bottom front of the engine cylinder. On the black-painted shift gate on the kneepad, the numbers 1 and 3 are picked out in white paint. (Doug Mitchel)

The same engine and transmission installation on a BMW R12 are seen from a different angle. On top of the engine block is the dynamo. The black, horizontally oriented cylinder above the rear of the transmission is the air cleaner. (Doug Mitchel)

On the right side of the R12 is the transmission gearshift lever, routed from the top of the transmission through the shift gate on the textured kneepad attached to the fuel tank. The diagonal tube to the front of the engine cylinder is a sidecar brace.

The passenger's right footboard on this R12 constitutes a metal base plate with a raised, rubber foot grip. Below it is the muffler, with a fishtail exhaust outlet. To the front of the rear footboard is the rear brake pedal. (Doug Mitchel)

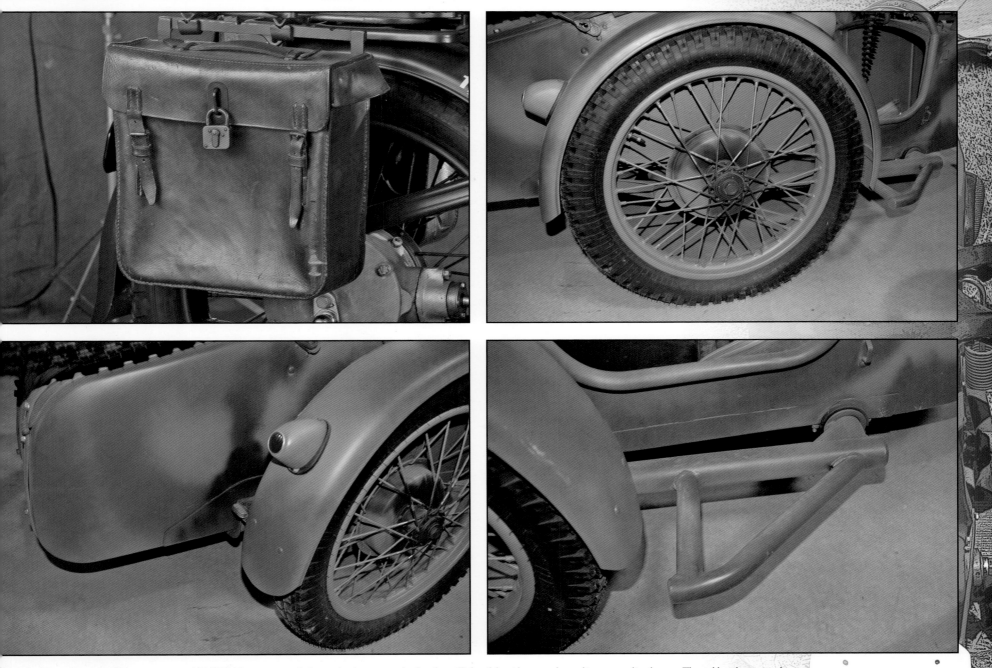

Top left: The right-rear saddlebag on a restored BMW R12 is constructed of russet leather and is equipped with two straps with buckles and a padlock hasp to secure the flap, and a leather carrying handle on top. The saddlebags were hung on brackets welded to the luggage rack. (Doug Mitchel) **Top right:** The sidecar wheel, disc brake, and tire of an R12 sidecar are shown in close-up. The operator's manual specified that the R12's tires were to show only light depression when the motorcycle was unloaded. **Above left:** Mounted on the rear of the fender, the taillight of the sidecar was housed in a streamlined cover. The red lens has vertical ridges. Between the tail light cover and the fender was a base plate. **Above right:** Protruding from the sidecar's frame to the front of the fender is an angled, tubular bumper, which served several purposes: it was a brush deflector, it helped protect the bottom of the fender from damage and it served as a step.

A view into the rear of an R12 sidecar reveals the wooden slats fastened to the floor. An MG 34 7.92mm machine gun is on a pintle mount, fastened to the tubular bar across the front deck of the sidecar.

Top left: This BMW R12 has been restored and painted in a dark-yellow and gray camouflage scheme. It features military-style fenders with metal-strap braces. The BMW logo is faintly visible on the frame adjacent to the fuel tank. **Top right:** The same BMW R12 is fitted with a sidecar and armed with an MG34. Toward the front of the sidecar's body are three raised, tapped fittings for attaching a saddlebag holder. **Above left:** In a rear view of the BMW R12 and sidecar combination, the lateral wooden slats on the floor of the sidecar are visible. The MG 34 is mounted on a pedestal attached to a lateral tube mounted above the top of the sidecar. **Above right:** The BMW R12 and sidecar are viewed from the front. A tan-colored saddlebag is clamped to a holder on the inboard side of the sidecar. (Roger Condron, all)

Top left: This photo of a BMW R12 provides a clear view of the headlight assembly, front wheel, forks, and handlebar, as well as details of the engine. Note the horn within the front end of the frame to the front of the engine. **Top right:** Elements of the frame connecting the sidecar to the BMW R12 are shown here, as well as details of the motorcycle's rear fender, taillight, and reflector. **Above left:** Although a rear seat is not installed on this BMW R12, footrests for a passenger are present. Note the speedometer set into the headlight case. **Above right:** Facing the R12 from the front, to the left on the handlebar are the front brake lever, throttle control/hand grip, headlight dimmer switch, and horn button. To the right are the clutch lever and hand grip/spark control. (Roger Condron, all)

Top left: One advantage of having a sidecar was it offered room for a spare tire. This spare was mounted on a basin-shaped bracket attached to the storage compartment door with eight hex screws. The round nut held the tire to the threaded spindle. **Top right:** The logo of the sidecar's manufacturer, Steib, is embossed in script on the side of the car. The three raised holes to the front of the car were for mounting a Y-shaped bracket for holding panniers and ammunition boxes. **Above left:** The pintle had teeth that engaged an elevation gear operated by a hand wheel, allowing the gun to be raised or lowered as necessary. The dark-colored bar to the front of the mount is a clamping handle, for tightening the mount on the crossbar. **Above right:** The handgrip on the right side of the handlebar of the BMW R12 also doubled as the throttle control. Mounted on the outer end of that grip is the brake lever. On the right side of the sidecar is the top of a leather pannier; the top part of its holder is visible.

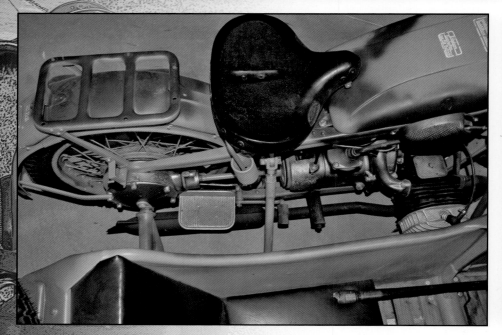

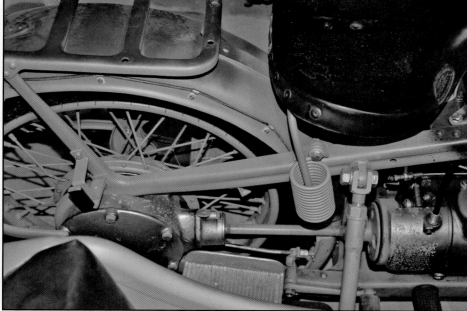

Top left: A downward view between the R12 motorcycle and the sidecar reveals the differential, disk brake, drive shaft (or Cardan shaft), right exhaust line and muffler, transmission, and gearshift. The luggage rack and passenger's footboard are also visible. **Top right:** The front of the driver's black leather saddle is hinged, while its rear is suspended on two coil springs. To the front of the spring is the rear brace for the sidecar frame. Attached with clips to the top of the fender is the taillight cable. **Above left:** The saddle bears the nameplate of the manufacturer, Drilastic, the corporate name of the Francke Brothers of Mühlhausen/Thüringen. The rivets around the rear of the saddle secured the rubber upholstery to the rear of the seat frame. **Above right:** Below the taillight on the R12 is a Wehrmacht license plate, and below the plate is a red reflector. At the bottom rear of the right side of the sidecar is a manufacturer's data plate. The leaf spring is visible along the sidecar.

BMW R35

Produced from 1937 to 1940, the BMW R35 medium motorcycle joined the BMW R4 as a training and courier vehicle in the Wehrmacht. It was a solo vehicle weighing 341 pounds unloaded, with a full fuel tank, and measured 78.74" long by 37.4" high by 31.5" wide. Some 15,386 R35s were manufactured in civilian and military versions, and from 1945 to the 1950s production resumed in East Germany, with over 34,000 being produced. Here, a German army motorcyclist poses on his R35.

In an overall view of the right side of an R35, the foot lever and pedal for the rear brake curves up from below the footrest. Incorporated into the front of the right knee rest is a gearshift gate.

The R35 featured a pressed-steel frame, designated the model 235, and a telescopic fork but lacked hydraulic damping. The rear suspension was rigid, and sprung saddles provided the driver and passenger with some relief from buffeting. The front tire was size 3.0-19 and the rear was 3.5-19.

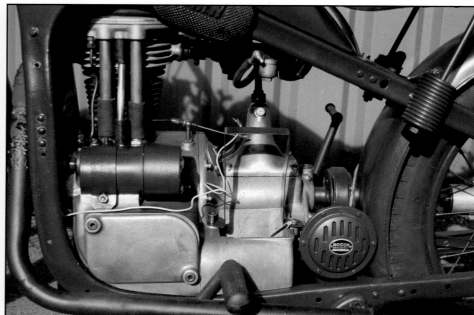

Top left: A canvas cover with a leather-lined blackout slot is fitted over the headlight, which in turn is fastened to brackets on top of the fork. At the very top of each side of the fork are oil filler plugs for the shock absorbers. **Top right:** On the left side of the handlebar are the clutch lever and spark control/hand grip. On the right side is the front brake lever and throttle control/hand grip. The wing nut to the front of the fuel filler cap with BMW logo is the steering damper. **Above left:** A speedometer/odometer is set into the headlight.

Although the speedometer goes to 120 kph, the maximum recommended speed was 100. Toward the top front of the light housing (outside of the photo) are the light switch, check light, and fuse holder. **Above right:** The 340cc engine had a single vertical cylinder and produced 14 horsepower at 3,500 rpm, with a compression ratio of 6.0:1. A side-facing Bosch horn is to the rear of the engine. Toward the bottom are the exhaust and the left footrest. This particular bike features the engine from an R4. (Ian Le Riche, all)

Both of the saddles on a BMW R35 motorcycle are viewed from the left side. The seats have almost a woven look, but the texture consists of regularly arranged, elongated-diamond shapes.

Top left: In view below the passenger's saddle are the luggage rack and its left support; the fender with the taillight and license plate; the springs of the front saddle; the passenger's footrests; and the left exhaust with its fishtail rear end. A clear view also is available of the rear of the left side of the frame. **Above left:** The rear of the fishtail-type exhaust port of the left muffler is depicted in close-up. The fishtail end piece is held onto the barrel of the muffler with a hex nut tightened onto a threaded shaft. (Ian Le Riche) **Right:** The sprung rear seat of the R35 straddles the luggage rack. The taillight is enclosed in a housing mounted on the rear of the fender. At the bottom of the fender are a license plate holder and a mud flap. On the left side of the vehicle is the fishtail muffler.

From this angle, a shadowed indentation is visible toward the rear of the fuel tank. This depression allowed clearance space for the front of the driver's saddle and its support. Tactical markings for a motorcycle platoon are on the rear fender and the side of the front fender.

The right side of the R35's engine and transmission are the focus of this photograph. Also in view are the rear-brake pedal and linkage, the passenger's right footrest in the raised position, the driver's right footrest, right kneepad and shift lever, and the right saddle spring.

Left: The R35 engine was a four-stroke, single-cylinder design with a displacement of 340cc. Ignition was by a Bosch magneto. The clutch was a single-plate, dry type. The four-speed transmission provided power to the differential by means of a shaft. The gearshift lever extended through the shift gate on the kneepad down to the top of the transmission. **Top right:** The right rear of the frame and the rigid rear suspension are shown. From the transmission (right), the drive shaft is linked to the aluminum-colored differential (left). Also in view are the rear brake lever (lower right) and link and the kick-starter. (Ian Le Riche) **Above right:** The R35 featured telescoping-fork front suspension and a pressed-steel twin-loop frame. The stencil "Atu." on the civilian-type fenders stands for atmosphärenüberdruck, or gauge pressure, a measure of air pressure above one bar. (Ian Le Riche)

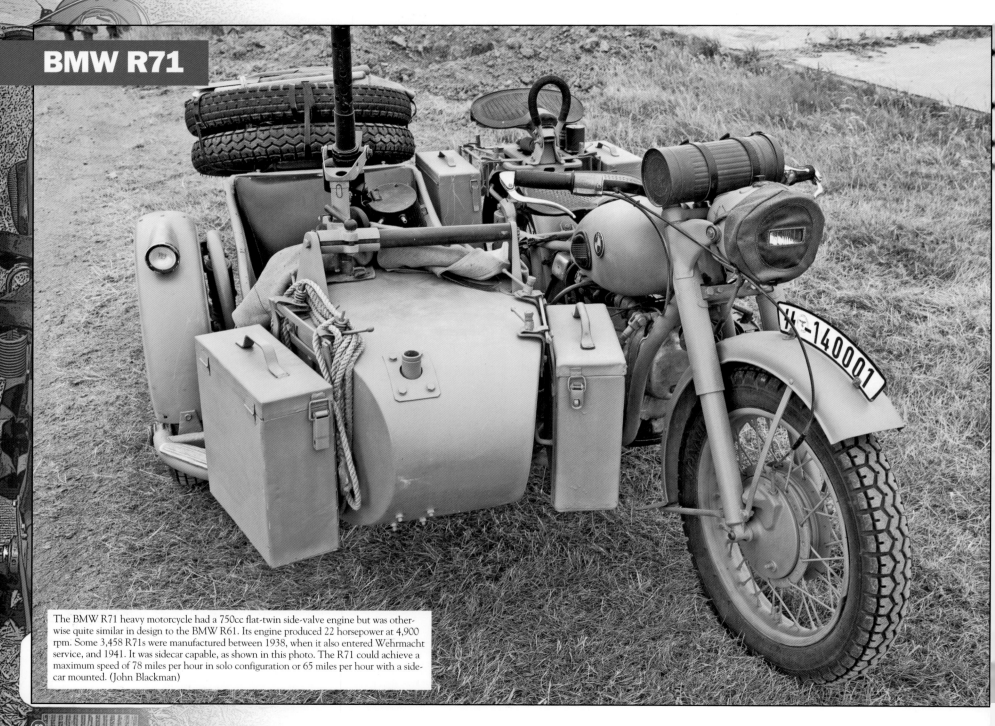

BMW R71

The BMW R71 heavy motorcycle had a 750cc flat-twin side-valve engine but was otherwise quite similar in design to the BMW R61. Its engine produced 22 horsepower at 4,900 rpm. Some 3,458 R71s were manufactured between 1938, when it also entered Wehrmacht service, and 1941. It was sidecar capable, as shown in this photo. The R71 could achieve a maximum speed of 78 miles per hour in solo configuration or 65 miles per hour with a sidecar mounted. (John Blackman)

The R71 mounted 3.5-19 tires. Like the R61, it had telescoping front and rear suspensions. It measured 83.85" long by 37.79" high by 32.08" wide, with a wheelbase of 55.11". Unloaded weight fully fueled was 410 pounds. (John Blackman)

At the bottom rear of the front fender and at a right angle to the fender was a small, flared mudguard. The kneepad on the side of the fuel tank was teardrop shaped, with a horizontally ridged texture. Above the transmission is the air cleaner. (John Blackman)

The taillight and its housing are mounted immediately above the rear license plate holder. Each of the metal panniers on the rear of the R71 is mounted on a bracket with a horizontal rod across the top. The rod rests on two hooks attached to the luggage rack and is locked in place by two swiveling locks. (John Blackman)

Two "potato masher" stick grenades are stowed between the luggage rack and the left pannier. Part of the rear differential is visible between the rear fender of the R71 and the right pannier. Strapped to the handlebar is a gas-mask container. (John Blackman)

Left: Atop the gasoline tank of the R71 are the fuel filler cap and the door to a toolbox enclosed in the tank. On the door is a placard with instructions and data on subjects such as tire pressure carburetor adjustment. Also included is a lubrication chart and diagram. (John Blackman)

Right: Details of the luggage rack and passenger's saddle of a BMW R71 are seen from the left rear. The saddle was buffered by a horizontal coil spring. The hinge for raising the rear of the fender is visible above the license plate and the taillight.

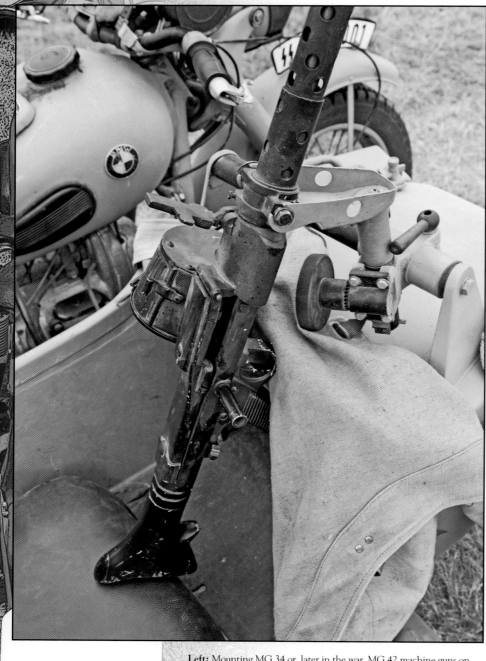

Left: Mounting MG 34 or, later in the war, MG 42 machine guns on sidecars gave a motorcycle unit an impressive array of firepower. These machine guns could be fired on the run, making the vehicles a much harder target to hit. (John Blackman, both)

SPECIFICATIONS

BMW R4	
Wheelbase	1.32 m
Weight	137 kg
Fuel capacity	12 liters
Maximum speed	100 km/hr
Engine configuration	1-cylinder, 4 stroke
Engine displacement	398 cc
Engine horsepower	12 @ 3500 rpm

BMW R12	
Wheelbase	1.38 m
Weight	185 kg
Fuel capacity	14 liters
Maximum speed	110 km/hr solo
Engine configuration	2-cylinder, 4 stroke
Engine displacement	740 cc
Engine horsepower	18 @ 3400 rpm

BMW R35	
Wheelbase	1.30 m
Weight	150 kg
Fuel capacity	12 liters
Maximum speed	100 km/hr
Engine configuration	1-cylinder, 4 stroke
Engine displacement	340 cc
Engine horsepower	14 @ 4500 rpm

BMW R71	
Wheelbase	1.40 m
Weight	187 kg
Fuel capacity	14 liters
Maximum speed	125 km/hr
Engine configuration	2-cylinder, 4 stroke
Engine displacement	746 cc
Engine horsepower	22 @ 4600 rpm

BMW R75	
Wheelbase	1.44 m
Weight	420 kg w/sidecar
Fuel capacity	24 liters
Maximum speed	92 km/hr with sidecar
Engine configuration	2-cylinder, 4 stroke, opposed piston
Engine displacement	745 cc
Engine horsepower	26 @ 4400 rpm

Zündapp KS 750	
Wheelbase	1.41 m
Weight	400 kg with sidecar
Fuel capacity	23 liters
Maximum speed	95 km/hr with sidecar
Engine configuration	2-cylinder, four-stroke, opposed piston
Engine displacement	751 cc
Engine horsepower	26 @ 4000 rpm

BMW R75

This BMW R75 and sidecar assigned to a Luftwaffe paratroop unit was an early-production motorcycle. It had an oil-bath air cleaner mounted on the transmission, rather than the later model with the felt air filter on top of the fuel tank.

The same R75's powered sidecar had a painting on the side of a Viking ship with "Norge" written on the sail. Equipment includes an MG 34 machine gun, leather pannier, and a waterproof cover that has been partially pulled to the side.

The crew of a BMW R75 motorcycle-sidecar combination pause on a height to survey a village somewhere on the Eastern Front. The vehicle has been painted in a subtle camouflage scheme. The license plate number is SS-162384. (NARA)

This BMW R75 and sidecar combination appears to be the same one shown in the preceding photograph. The "SS" part of the license plate above the front fender is visible. The BMW logo plate on the frame below the fuel tank is in its original colors and has not been painted over. (NARA)

Four Fallschirmjägers, including a driver wearing motorcycle gauntlets, are poised on a BMW R75 and sidecar during the retreat from Normandy. The extra men, gear and spare tires have probably exceeded the capacity of this small vehicle. This photo was taken in the town of Bourgtheroulde, France in late August 1944. (NARA)

A trooper takes a snooze in the sidecar of a BMW R75. On the sidecar is the insignia of the 1st Cavalry Division and its successor after late 1941, the 24th Panzer Division. License plate WH-1046064 is on the fender. Below it is the tactical symbol for a motorcycle unit. Caution stripes are painted on the edge of the sidecar fender and brace. (NARA)

A restored R75 exhibits its sidecar. A steel pannier is latched to both racks on the front of the car. On the right fender below the sidecar's headlight is a painted-over BMW logo plate. An MG 34 is mounted in the elevating pintle mount.

Another R75 with a sidecar, this time with a non-painted BMW logo plate. Among the sidecar's accessories are an elevating pintle mount for the machine gun (not installed) and a canvas door. The motorcycle and sidecar are painted Dunkelgelb (dark yellow).

The same vehicle was photographed from the front left. On the front of the sidecar is the symbol of the 9th Panzer Division.

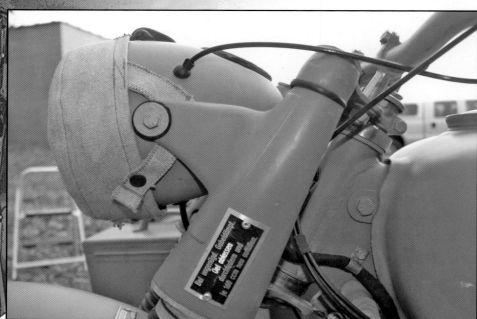

Top left: The R75 was fitted with 4.5-16 off-road tires. The front drum brakes were 9.84" in diameter. Below the Bosch horn at the top of the frame, the generator protrudes from the front of the engine block. **Top right:** The telescoping front suspension incorporated coil springs and oil shock absorbers. Late-model R75s had rubber sleeves on the midsections of both sides of the fork, to keep out dust and dirt. The tow hook below the horn is on the side-car frame. **Above left:** A plate on the side of the fork gives instructions on maintaining the oil in the shock absorbers: each side of the fork had a capacity of .16 liters. The headlight and its canvas blackout cover are also emphasized in this view. **Above right:** When folded in the stored position, the bottom of the front kickstand, or crutch, was secured with wing nuts to a turned-back flange at the bottom of the front fender. When thus stored, the kickstand also acted as a fender brace.

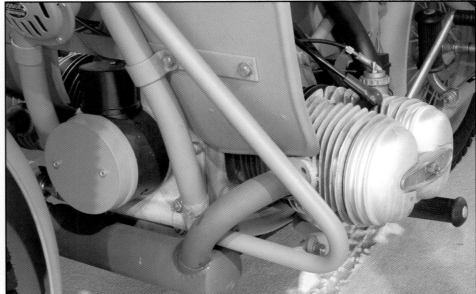

Top left: Tubular safety guards were installed on this R75; at the top center, above the Bosch horn, is the point where the left guard was fastened to the frame with a hex nut. Details of the fender bracket are also visible. **Top right:** The R75 had a front muffler (bottom left) in addition to the muffler to the right rear of the motorcycle. Above the front muffler is the generator. To the upper center is a sheet metal leg guard, an optional accessory. **Above left:** The fuel tank, wearing the symbol of the Afrika Korps, had a capacity of 6.34 U.S. gallons (with .79 gallon in reserve). Protruding from the top of the tank are the filler cap and the cover for the felt air filter. **Above right:** The overall arrangement of the left side of the R75 from the front of the frame to the rear is illustrated. The frame was of tubular, bolted construction, with a rigid rear suspension. Within the heart of the frame is the 745cc engine.

Top left: The design of the left cylinder and head is exhibited. To the rear of each cylinder were Graetzin SA 24/1 (left) and SA 24/2 (right) carburetors. The air intakes were routed from the air cleaner housed in the fuel tank, to the carburetors. **Top right:** Proper and timely lubrication was essential to the dependability of any military motorcycle. Affixed to the rear of the left leg guard is a lubrication chart for the R75 and sidecar. To the upper right is the painted-over BMW logo plate. **Above left:** At the bottom is the driver's left footrest, with the transmission shift foot pedal to the front of it. The black box next to the transmission is the 7-amp battery, secured in place with a clamp-type bracket with a tightening thumbscrew at top. **Above right:** To the immediate rear of the battery is the kick-starter, below which is the kickstand, shown in its folded-up position. Mounted on the frame to the rear of the kick-starter is the folded-up rear passenger's right footrest.

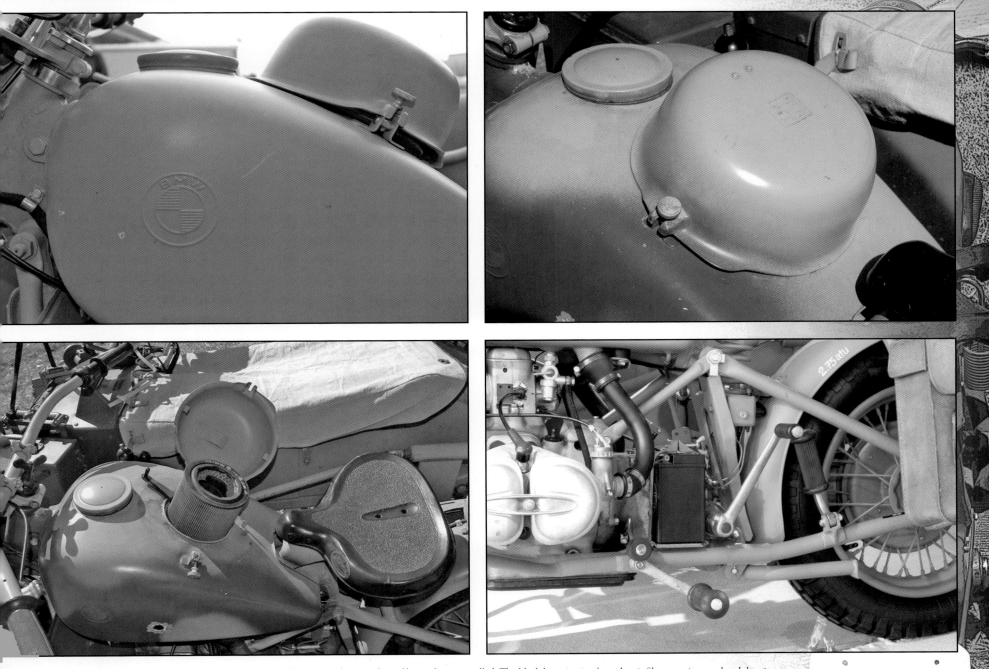

Top left: The fuel tank is viewed from the left side. On top of it is the filler cap, to the rear of which is the cover for the air cleaner. By loosening the thumbscrew on the side, the cover could be raised, exposing the felt air filter for cleaning. **Top right:** The felt air filter located beneath the cover was shaped like a cylindrical bellows. To clean it, it was removed from a perforated mount and shaken out. Unfiltered air entered the filter from the gap under the cover by the thumbscrew. **Above left:** With the cover open, a non-original replacement air filter is shown installed. The black lever issuing from the air filter opening regulated the air inlet opening; it was pushed to the right when starting the engine and to the left when the engine was warm. **Above right:** The area from the left side of the engine to the rear wheel, including the foot shift pedal, is shown on a different R75. Transmission shifting was effected either through the foot shift pedal or the hand shift levers on the right side of the fuel tank.

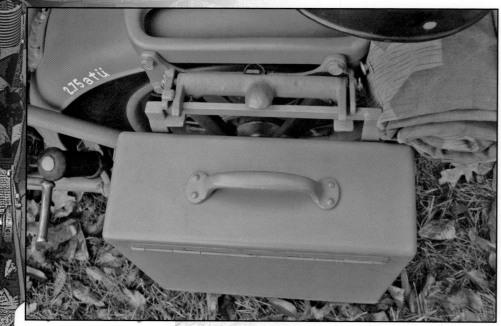

Top left: A stitched leather pannier is fastened to the holder over the rear fender. The white stencil "2.75 Atü." refers to the recommended gauge pressure of the rear tire. The specified gauge pressure for the front tire was 1.75. **Top right:** On this R75, a sheet metal pannier is fastened to bracket over the rear fender. Projecting over the rear fender and taillight was a lifting loop, for manhandling the rear of the motorcycle into position when necessary. **Above left:** A downward view of a metal pannier shows the riveted handle and piano hinge for the lid. The clamping-type bracket that holds the pannier is bolted to the luggage rack, which also supports the passenger's saddle. **Above right:** Like the BMW R61 and R71, the R75 had a hinged rear fender, to facilitate changing the tire. To the right of the fender is the rear muffler with its perforated guard, beyond which is a tubular frame with a trailer hitch.

A view of a different R75 with sidecar emphasizes the wide fuel tank with the prominent air filter on top, and the arrangement of the tandem saddles. The R75's tubular, multi-part frame facilitated replacing damaged parts.

The sidecar wheel was driven by a transverse driveshaft attached to the motorcycle's wheel drive. This driveshaft passed under the sidecar and was connected to a swing-arm gearbox on the right side of the car, which drove the sidecar wheel.

Left: The trailer-hitch accessory is shown in detail. The R75 with sidecar had sufficient power to pull a small trailer for carrying ammunition and other supplies. To the left is the muffler; its guard was attached to the muffler by screws through tabs in the guard.

Right: Another R75 with sidecar displays a trailer hitch. At the rear end of the hitch assembly is a simple hook with a retainer pin, mounted on a universal joint. Also in view is the Drilastic nameplate fastened to the rear of the passenger's saddle.

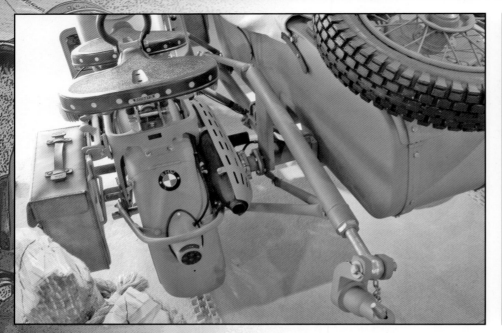

Top left: The front end of the main horizontal arm of the hitch was attached to a vertical leg, the bottom of which was fastened to the sidecar axle housing. A series of tubular braces gave additional rigidity to the hitch assembly. **Top right:** The attachment point of the vertical leg of the hitch to the axle housing is shown, as well as the two rear tubular braces of the hitch. To the left of the bottom of the leg are the flanges attaching the sidecar axle housing to the motorcycle's wheel drive. **Above left:** The sidecar axle passes through a circular cutout at the bottom of the leg of the hitch, which in turn is fastened to the flange on the axle housing with six bolts and nuts. The rear braces of the hitch are bolted to the bottom of the leg and the motorcycle frame. **Above right:** Details in this view of the rear end of an R75 include the rear latch for the lid of the pannier, the hinge on the foldable rear fender, the painted-over BMW logo plate, the taillight assembly and cable, and Wehrmacht license plate.

Top left: The wheel drive and hydraulic drum brake of an R75 are shown in close-up without the trailer-hitch assembly present. The sidecar axle is attached to the wheel drive to the right of the exhaust (the dark-colored tube at center). **Top right:** The sidecar axle and the configuration of its attachment to the wheel drive are shown from a different angle. At the upper center is the left leaf spring of the sidecar, to the left of which are the two adjustable diagonal braces of the sidecar. **Above left:** The sidecar axle housing is viewed from underneath the right rear of a sidecar. To the far left of the axle is the leg supporting the trailer hitch assembly, and the rear of the underside of the sidecar is at the top left. **Above right:** The sidecar axle/wheel-drive attachment is illustrated on a BMW R75 without a trailer hitch assembly installed. The left leaf spring of the sidecar is above and to the front of the sidecar axle. The diagonal braces were of adjustable, telescoping design.

Strapped onto this R75 is a variety of combat gear, including "potato masher" hand grenades and a spade. The spare tire is wearing a chain, for better traction in snow or mud. Above the 9th Panzer Division symbol is a BMW nameplate.

Top left: A view of the right rear of a sidecar offers a peek at the rear of the right leaf spring, mounted to a bearing on a cradle that passes underneath the frame. Below the spare tire are the hinges and steel reinforcing straps for the storage compartment door. **Top right:** A modern Engelbrecht 120-16 off-road tire is stowed on the sidecar. The large, gray nut on the threaded spindle holds the hub in place. Wheel spokes required regular inspection to make sure they remained taut. **Above left:** The wheel of the spare tire included a drum brake and could be used on any of the three wheel mountings of the R75 and its sidecar. The placard affixed to the fender of the sidecar reads, "swing arm / lubricate weekly." **Above right:** The wheel spokes of the spare tire offered a convenient means of strapping down extra equipment, such as the stick grenades, spade, spare machine gun barrel container, gas mask canister, and rolled tarp.

Top left: The right rear spring bearing of an R75 sidecar is shown in close-up. A grease fitting is located on top of the bearing. To the front of the spring bearing is a tunnel in the bottom of the sidecar body, to provide clearance to the axle. **Top right:** Leather straps on a canvas cover are fastened to studs on the body of the sidecar. The unpainted metal handle next to the corner of the canvas cover operated a rod inside the storage compartment that released the internal latches of the door. **Above left:** The spare tire on this R75 sidecar has a similar off-road tread pattern to a type used on German heavy motorcycles during World War II. Below the tire is its mounting bracket. The rear of the trailer hitch is visible in profile. **Above right:** The latch handle for the storage compartment door is painted the same dark yellow as the surrounding areas of this R75 sidecar. Note the rolled edge of the passenger's door and the studs for attaching a canvas cover over the passenger's compartment. (Chris Hughes)

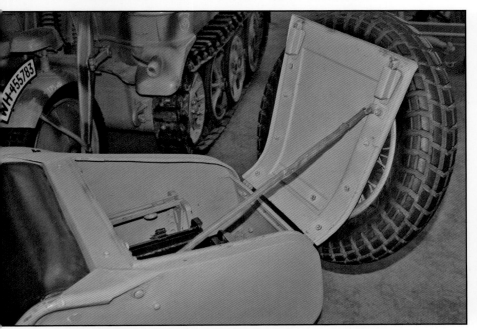

Top left: The inside of the storage compartment door had a pressed steel border, for added strength. The eight nuts and bolts on the left and right sides of the door secured the reinforcing straps and the spare tire bracket. The two latches are at the top. **Top right:** The storage compartment provided space to carry extra ammunition and equipment. Here, a Gurttrommeltrager, a carrying rack for two 50-round 7.92mm ammunition magazines, sits atop three 50-round Patronenkasten (ammunition boxes). **Above left:** Attached to the locking handle for the storage compartment door was a rod with a cam on each side. When the door was closed and the handle turned, the cams released the sprung latches, allowing the door to be opened. **Above right:** From this angle, another Gurttrommeltrager, painted Dunkelgelb, is visible in the storage compartment. The orange hold-open cord is not original equipment. The extra reinforcing on the door alleviated the stresses caused by the weight of the spare tire. (Chris Hughes, all)

Left: The open door to the storage compartment is viewed from the front, with the top of the sidecar passenger's seat at the bottom. The freely sliding bolts of the sprung latches exhibit paint chipping where they have made metal-on-metal contact. (Chris Hughes) **Top right:** Details of the sidecar wheel and tire and fender are provided. The leaf spring is visible through the spokes. Also visible in profile are the taillight and headlight assemblies. The tire's recommended gauge pressure is stenciled on the fender. **Above right:** This R75 sidecar has provisions for storing a spade, using a bracket to hold the blade and a clamp to secure the handle. On the fender is the plate reminding the crew to lubricate the swing arm weekly.

The standardized sidecar with driven wheel was introduced in 1942 for use with suitably equipped heavy motorcycles. However, in 1944, production on sidecar motorcycles ceased, with emphasis being shifted to the cheaper Kübelwagen.

1.75 atü

211746

Top left: The sidecar passenger's seat, spare tire, and fender are viewed to the rear. Note the small triangular gussets at the corners of the bodywork above the corners of the seat back. Also in view are the muffler shield and passenger's saddle. **Top right:** Looking down at the sidecar fender reveals the cables for the headlight and the BMW plate. On the inside of the fender is the fender bracket, an L-shaped tube secured to the frame with two U-bolts, which also secure the front of the spring to the frame. **Above left:** The standardized side-cars with driven wheel had an angled guard on the frame next to the door. This one has been wrapped with twine. Below the front of the door is the right side of the tunnel, below which the front of the frame passes under the body. **Above right:** The front of the fender is attached to the frame with a bracket. At the upper center, the fender bracket and front of the leaf springs are secured to the sidecar frame with two U-bolts through a bracket welded to the top of the frame.

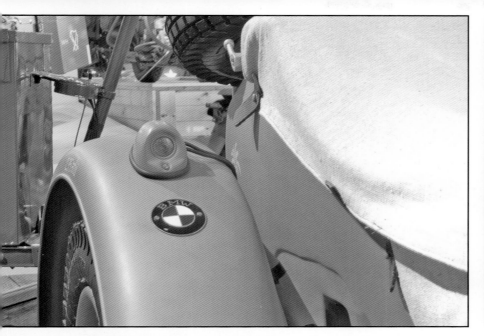

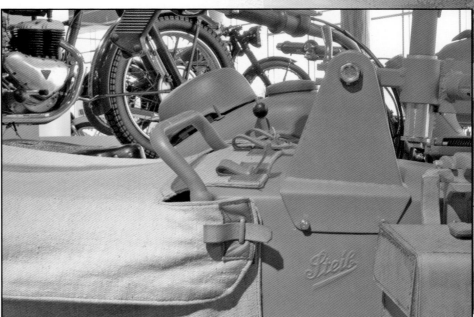

Top left: A view of the front of the sidecar reveals the design of the headlight assembly, including a clear lens in a housing, mounted on a dark-colored base plate. Note the slightly raised rim around the edge of the fender. **Top right:** Although slight in size and construction, the canvas door helped prevent mud and water from splashing into the sidecar. It was attached with straps through footman loops at the front and with quick-release straps secured to studs at the rear. **Above left:** Although BMW branded R75 sidecars with its nameplate, other manufacturers supplied parts and components. The name of the maker of this body, Steib, is embossed to the front of the door. Details of the leather pannier are also visible. **Above right:** The top cover installed on this sidecar overlaps the canvas door and includes cutouts for the handhold. The design of the right bracket of the machine gun mounting tube is displayed, along with the pintle mount and elevating gear.

Inside an R75 sidecar, the wooden slats attached to the floor are visible.

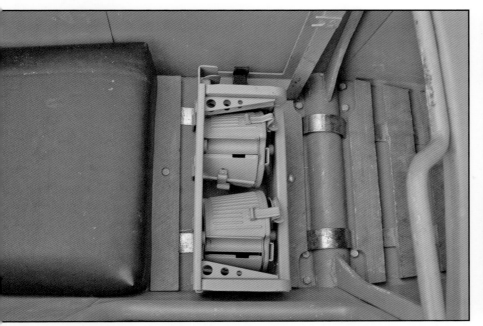

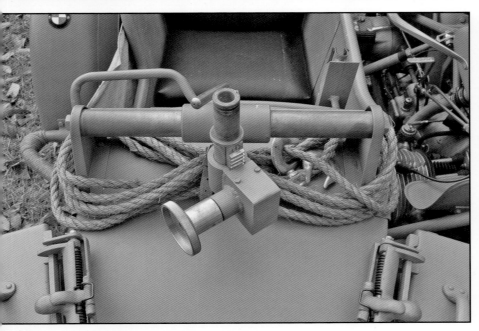

Top left: To the front of the seat on the floor of this sidecar is a carrying rack for two 50-round 7.92mm ammunition magazines for an MG 34. To the front of the rack is the tunnel for the front cross member of the frame. **Top right:** The bare metal mounting bar for the pintle mount had a ridge across the back of it. As can be seen in this photo, that ridge acted as a stop to keep the clamp-type base of the pintle mount from inadvertently rotating back and forth. **Above left:** At the front of the mount is a carriage with an elevating gear,

operated by the small hand wheel. Visible on the socket of the mount are teeth, which engaged with the elevating gear to raise or lower the machine gun as required. **Above right:** An MG 34 is installed on its mount. As can be seen from the shiny metal at the bottom of the pintle, the elevation gear allowed only a few inches of upward movement of the mount, but this could be just enough to give the gunner the necessary play.

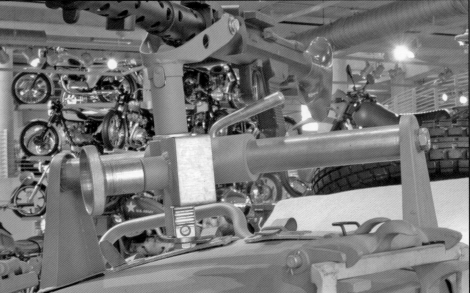

Left: The elevating gear, hand wheel, and cradle-and-pintle assembly are shown close-up. To the rear of the pintle is a handle that tightened or loosened the mount, allowing the gun to be shuttled side to side for the convenience of the gunner. **Top right:** As viewed from the left front side of the sidecar, the teeth on the pintle are visible below the gearbox. To the lower right, details of the pannier rack are available. Note how the jaws of the rack clamp the unpainted metal frame of the pannier in place. **Above right:** Sighting down the barrel of an MG 34 from the front, in the foreground is the muzzle cone assembly and front sight, followed by the perforated cooling jacket over the barrel. The ring around the barrel held a ring sight for antiaircraft use.

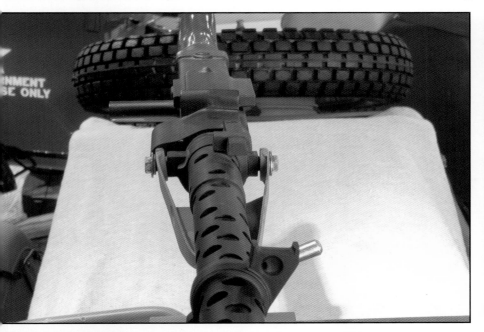

Top left: The mount for the ring sight and the trunnions are shown in close-up. Above the barrel between the trunnions is what appears to be a mock rear sight. To the rear is the top of the receiver and the stock. **Top right:** A close-up of the MG 34's muzzle cone assembly, which incorporated a flash suppressor, also affords a clear view of the tops of the pannier racks. These racks had small release levers; there was another design of rack that had handles with ball knobs. **Above left:** On the front of this R75 sidecar is the swastika and palm tree symbol of the Afrika Korps. The tactical symbol painted below it stands for a motorized company headquarters. Further details of the pannier racks are visible. **Above right:** The front end of a different R75 exhibits a bolted-on sheet metal plate and a bullet-hole decal. This type of nose was referred to as a "hammer" design. Leather straps through footman loops proved a simple but effective way to secure the canvas cover.

A BMW R75 motorcycle/sidecar is viewed from the front. The panniers fastened to the front of the sidecar were fabricated from sheet steel. The pannier on the right side of the sidecar has a padlock through the latch.

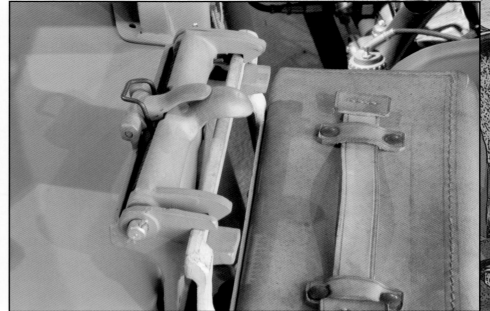

Top left: A towrope is looped around the brackets of the machine gun mount. A tow hook was provided on the front of the frame of the R75 sidecars (out of view) for rapidly hooking on a towrope to retrieve the vehicle if it became mired. **Top right:** Shown here in close-up, the metal frame of the pannier was secured to the rack on the sidecar with a large clamp with a claw on each end. Pulling back on the small lever at the top center of the rack released the clamping action, allowing removal of the pannier. **Above left:** The stitched construction of a tanned leather pannier is illustrated. The straps are leather, with metal buckles. Just visible below the pannier is the tow hook mounted on the sidecar frame. Details of the R75's front fender and fork are also visible. **Above right:** The license plate was sandwiched between two pairs of brackets on the front fender and fastened with screws and nuts. To the left is one of the two wing nuts and screws that secure the bottom of the front kickstand to the fork.

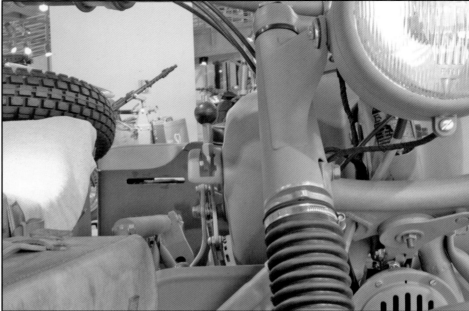

Top left: Mounted on the side of the fuel tank are a manual transmission shift lever (closest to the fuel tank) and a lever (pointing to the front) for selecting off-road gearing. Using the latter lever decreased the gear ratios for better off-road performance. **Top right:** The manual shift gate (center) is viewed from the front of the R75. Either the hand-shift lever or the foot shift pedal could be used to change gears. The hand shifter also acted as a gear-position indicator. **Above left:** To the rear of the shift gate (upper right) is the bearing where the rear telescoping sidecar brace is attached to the R75's frame. The nut and threaded shaft on the brace allowed it to be adjusted for length. The right carburetor is to the lower right. **Above right:** The differential lock could be engaged with the lever at center to transition the R75 to rigid-axle drive, for better handling on soft or slippery surfaces. Also visible are the manual shift link rods, rear-wheel drive, and muffler guard.

Top left: The hand shift levers and links are viewed looking straight down. This view also provides a good look at the right cylinder, top of the carburetor, right leg guard, and the two telescoping, adjustable sidecar braces and their manner of attachment to the frame. **Above left:** The handlebar, fuel tank, fork, and headlight are viewed from the right side. In the upper left foreground are the throttle control/hand grip and hand brake lever for the front wheel brake. **Right:** A museum BMW R75 with powered sidecar is viewed from the front. At the forward end of the fender is the front lifting loop, similar to the lifting loop fitted to the rear fender. On top of the fender are the small brackets for a license plate, not installed.

Top left: A blackout cover is fastened over the headlight of this R75. Note how the cover is cut out around the switch on top of the light housing. The horn is visible below the headlight, and above the cylinders are the leg guards. **Top right:** The speedometer on top of the headlight housing was graduated in kilometers per hour, with a top speed of 100 (62 miles per hour). The scale on this speedometer reads clockwise. An odometer is above the needle.

Above left: A close-up of the left side of the handlebar shows the clutch lever and the handgrip. On the bar to the side of the grip are the headlight dimmer switch and the horn button. **Above right:** The right side of the handlebar of an R75 is depicted, showing the hand lever for the front brake and the hand grip/throttle control. Also in view are the right side of the air filter cover (top right) and the inside of the sidecar.

Top left: The felt air filter on top of the fuel tank was an early modification to the R75 based on lessons learned during motorcycle operations in North Africa. On the rear of the passenger's saddle is the Drilastic nameplate. **Top right:** To the upper right of the air filter cover is the small lever for regulating the air inlet size, to richen or lean-out the fuel mixture. To the right of the saddle is the brass-colored differential lock lever, with "SPERREN" (lock) embossed on the handle. **Above left:** On the right side of the driver and passenger's saddles is an oval embossing with the Drilastic logo. The design of the passenger's saddle is also highlighted, including the coil spring under the saddle. **Above right:** In a tandem seating arrangement, the luggage rack served as a mounting platform for the passenger's saddle as well as a pannier. The oval, embossed Drilastic logo is repeated on the left side of both saddles.

Zündapp KS750

Following an extensive development and testing phase, the Zündapp KS750 heavy motorcycle made its debut in May 1941, with significant numbers entering combat by the fall of that year and approximately 18,635 units ultimately being delivered by the end of the war. The vehicle featured a locking differential, reverse drive, and a driven sidecar. At the heart of the KS750 was a powerful 751cc overhead-valve, opposed-twin engine. Here, troops from a Wehrmacht motorcycle reconnaissance unit in tropical uniforms pose by their KS750s. (NARA)

Waffen-SS troops gather around a Zündapp KS750 heavy motorcycle with a driven sidecar, most likely during a training exercise. An unusual type of handlebar is present, with a separate bar mounted below, and attached to, the stock handlebar, apparently for reinforcement. (NARA)

A full complement of three men is on this KS750. This motorcycle also has the extra bar underneath the stock handlebar. This model of Zündapp motorcycle entered service in May 1941, just in time for the invasion of the Soviet Union. (NARA)

A restored KS750 sports an MG 34 with drum magazine on the sidecar's pintle mount and a nonstandard Notek blackout light on the front of the sidecar. Big, off-road tires with heavy lugs were mounted, size 4.6-16. The license plate lacks numbers.

The KS750 introduced a new design of fork of welded construction. It was attached to the steering mechanism with four articulated links. There was only one muffler, and it was next to the rear wheel.

Top left: Each engine cylinder was angled 5 degrees above horizontal. A two-piece cover was installed over the engine block. The KS750 had a maximum speed of 58.9 miles per hour with a sidecar attached. Wheelbase was 55.51". **Top right:** The cover atop the engine block hides from view the Solex 30BRFH carburetor and Bosch FJ2R carburetor. The black-painted head covers are the plain, late-model type. To the front of the driver's footrest is the foot gearshift pedal. **Above left:** The fuel tank fits between the upper runs of the frame and had a capacity of six gallons. A toolbox was incorporated into the fuel tank. The driver's saddle was suspended on two coil springs. The battery is to the front of the kick starter. **Above right:** The early-type ribbed head covers are present on this museum KS750. The horn is mounted at the upper front of the frame; its rear and wiring are visible. A footrest is mounted on the bottom of the fork.

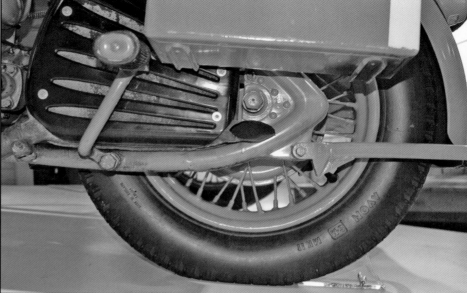

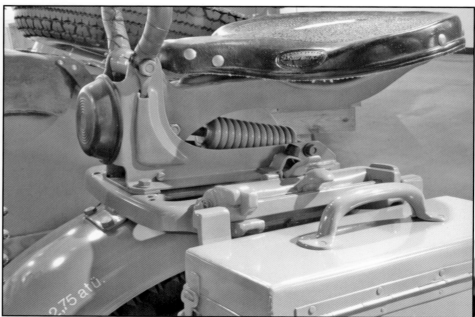

Top left: The battery, kick-starter, and muffler and its guard are shown in close-up. Note the screw-clamp holder for the battery and the tab on the muffler attached with a hex screw to the fender. **Top right:** The rear suspension was rigid. Next to the muffler is the passenger's left footrest. Attached to the rear of the frame is the rear kickstand. Details of the underside of the metal pannier are also visible. **Above left:** The metal pannier has a fixed handle on the lid and a piano hinge. In addition to holding the pannier, the heavy-duty luggage rack also supports the passenger's saddle. The recommended gauge pressure for the rear tire, 2.75, is painted on the fender. **Above right:** The passenger's saddle was cushioned by a horizontal spring. Drilastic manufactured the saddle. The round rubber object projecting from the front of the saddle frame was a bumper, to limit the rearward motion of the driver's saddle.

This KS750 is equipped with a trailer hitch assembly. It comprised a horizontal tube with a tow hook on a universal joint, supported by braces attached to the motorcycle's frame. Note also the hinged rear fender.

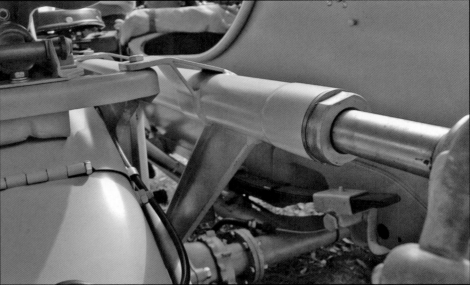

Top left: The hook of the trailer hitch is shown in close-up. The crooked pin inserted through a hole in the hook acted as a retainer. The universal joint allowed the trailer to flex on irregular ground without putting undue stress on the hitch. **Top right:** The horizontal tube to the front of the tow hook is shown. At the center is the support bracket of the trailer hitch, which was attached to the right rear of the KS750's frame. A bracket welded to the tube is fastened to the right rear of the luggage rack. **Above left:** The KS750's trailer hitch is shown with the tow bar of a trailer (left) secured to the tow hook. While the trailer hitch of the BMW R75 was supported by a leg attached to the sidecar axle, brackets attached to the frame and luggage rack supported this hitch. **Above right:** A trailer tow bar is shown attached to the tow hook. The retainer pin of the hook is equipped with a retainer chain. The pin securing the hook assembly to the ball joint is fastened with a cotter pin.

A rear view of a KS750-sidecar combination illustrates how close to the motorcycle the trailer hitch was positioned. The BMW R75's trailer hitch, by comparison, was positioned more equally between the sidecar and motorcycle.

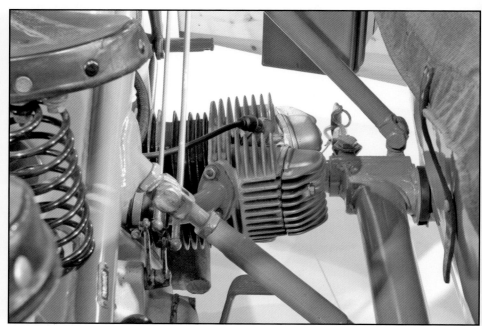

Top left: The taillight and its electrical cables are viewed from above. The taillight assembly was mounted on a gasket, to help keep out moisture. The shape of the rear kickstand is also illustrated. **Top right:** The sidecar axle of the KS750 was developed by Zündapp, and the design was also used for the BMW R75 sidecar axle. Its manner of attachment to the wheel drive is shown. Note how the rear kickstand is secured to the fender with a nut and bolt. **Above left:** The bottom of the rear diagonal brace of the sidecar was fastened to a saddle bracket on the left side of the sidecar frame. The braces were telescoping assemblies and could be adjusted to properly align the sidecar. **Above right:** The upper end of the sidecar brace was fastened to an attachment on the frame. To the upper right is the attachment point of the front sidecar brace to the sidecar frame. The two rods to the right of the saddle are links to the hand gear shifters.

A small trailer is hitched to a KS750-sidecar combination. The sidecar exhibits its hydraulic brake, spare tire, MG 34 machine gun with drum magazine, leather pannier, and canvas side door.

The spare tire on the sidecar of the KS750 is stored on a threaded spindle and secured with a hex nut. The motorcycle and the sidecar have matching taillight assemblies. On the left side of the fender of the sidecar is the fender support.

Top left: A bread bag with a canteen attached is strapped to the spare tire spindle. Below the spare tire are the hinges of the storage compartment door. On the sidecar fender is the tail light assembly and electrical cable. **Top Right:** Notek blackout lights were not ordinarily mounted on sidecars. A close-up view is provided of the clamping-type brackets for the panniers. Note the cotter pins securing the hinge pins of the brackets. **Above left:** The fully enclosed front disk brake was of mechanical operation, whereas the rear and sidecar brakes were hydraulic. The L-shaped support frame of a metal pannier mounted on the sidecar is also visible. **Above right:** On each side of the front wheel of this KS750 are spindle-shaped objects that the parts manuals called "*Raste (zur Vorderradachse)*," which sometimes are seen in photos of this model of motorcycle. They were somewhat tubular in shape with lateral grooves in them.

In addition to the canvas door, a rolled-up canvas cover is at the front of the passenger's opening on the sidecar. An entrenching tool is strapped to the bar of the machine gun mount.

Details of the interior of the sidecar of a KS750 are evident, along with features on the motorcycle, such as the speedometer on the headlight housing, the toolbox lid on top of the fuel tank, the gear-shifting levers and linkages, the saddles, and the passenger's grab handle.

On the side of the sidecar to the rear of the right pannier is the manufacturer's stamp, Steib, in raised script. On the floor of the sidecar is a lateral, tubular frame section. Welded to the left side of the tube is a vertical rib with a flared bottom, part of the frame of the sidecar body.

The KS750 and sidecar are viewed from the front with a small trailer hitched. A canvas blackout cover is strapped over the headlight. The footrests attached to the bottom of the front fork are also visible.

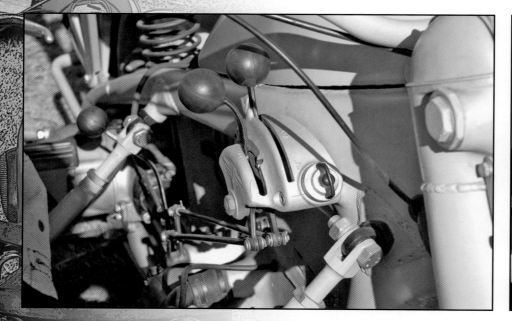

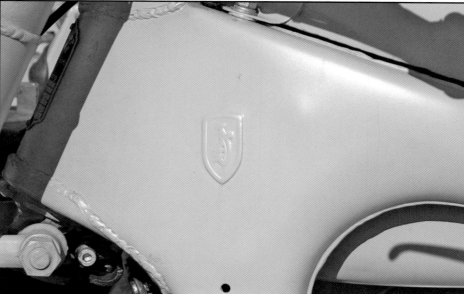

Top left: Changing gears was effected through a foot pedal or this combination of hand shift levers. The lever closest to the fuel tank was the transmission shift, while the other lever selected on- or off-road range. The ignition switch is on the front of the housing. **Top right:** The Zündapp corporate logo was stamped on the upper front of each side of the frame. Above the logo is a bolt securing the fuel tank to the frame. Note the welded seams on the frame and the fork (upper left). **Above left:** Set into the 6-gallon fuel tank was a toolbox with lid. On top of each side of the fork was a removable cover held down by a wire bail. To the far left is the headlight, with a speedometer incorporated into the housing. **Above right:** The lever on the handlebar to the driver's right was for the front brake, while the lever on the opposite side of the handlebar was for the clutch. The knurled knob at the center top of the handlebar was the steering damper.

A Zündapp KS750 is configured to tow an IF8 cart modified as a trailer. Features worthy of notice are the Notek blackout headlight on the upper front of the sidecar, the MG 34 machine gun with ammunition drum on a pedestal mount on the sidecar, and the canvas blackout cover on the service headlight of the KS750.

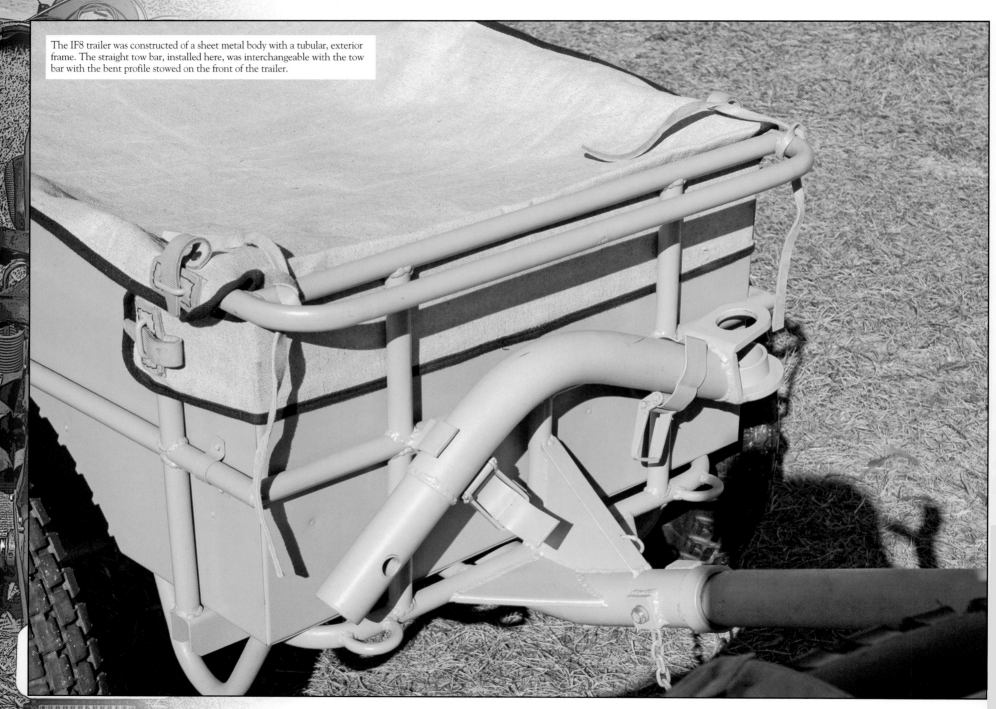

The IF8 trailer was constructed of a sheet metal body with a tubular, exterior frame. The straight tow bar, installed here, was interchangeable with the tow bar with the bent profile stowed on the front of the trailer.

The wheels were mounted to offset, crank-type spindle assemblies with shock absorbers attached. Empty weight of the IF8 trailer was 180 pounds, while the load capacity was 772 pounds.

Left: An IF8 trailer with external tubular frame is unhitched from the KS750 and tilted back, offering a view of the underside. These trailers were put to use hauling ammunition and other essential stores. **Top right:** This is a different type of small trailer, with embossed stiffeners in the sheet metal of the body instead of an external frame. The top of the right shock absorber was attached to a bracket at the top of two vertical frame members. **Above right:** Attached to the rear of the frame of the trailer was a tow hook for hitching an extra trailer. A retainer pin, shown lying against the body of the trailer, was inserted through the hole in the hook to hold the tow bar of the following trailer in place.

Top left: Details of the inner side of the left wheel of an IF8 trailer and its connection to the [of]fset spindle are displayed. Attached to two brackets cast into the axle assembly is the bot-[to]m of a shock absorber. **Top right:** The inside of the right wheel is depicted. The frame [u]nder the trailer body consists of channel-type cross members and longitudinal rods. The [la]rge pipe to the right supports the tow bar to the front and a tandem hitch to the rear. **[A]bove left:** The IF8 trailer is seen from the front, with its rear resting on the ground. The

bent tow bar is stowed on the front by means of two clamps. The selected tow bar was secured to the pipe running under the trailer by the bent pin fitted with a retainer chain. **Above right:** The tow bar of an IF8, right, is hitched to the tow pintle attachment on a motorcycle. There has been some debate over how common it was for German military motorcycles to tow trailers during World War II, with evidence indicating that aside from experimental trailer rigs, the practice was not widespread.

A restored Zündapp KS750 has an IF8 trailer hitched to it. The IF8 was designed as a cart, to be pulled by human or animal power. Above the right tire of the trailer can be seen the top of the right shock absorber and its mounting bracket.